Maïte Roche

 # The Bible
for little children

CTS Children's Books

Maïte Roche

The Bible
for little children

In the beginning, God made heaven and earth. God made the light which shines. He made the trees and the different fruits, the sun, the moon and the stars, the fish, the birds and all the animals. God made man and woman in his image. He blessed them and said, "Fill the earth. I give it to you". And God saw that it was good.

God said to Adam and Eve, "Everything in my garden is good for you, except the fruit of the tree which gives knowledge of good and evil. Do not eat it!" The evil serpent said, "You should eat it! It's delicious!" Adam and Eve ate the fruit. They had disobeyed God. What a terrible mistake! They had to leave the garden. But God stayed with them on their journey.

God's friend,
Noah, went in
his ark with his
family and all the
animals.
There was water
everywhere
because God
wanted to make
a new world.
When God
stopped the rain,
the flood was
over and life
started again.
God said,
"The rainbow
will be the
sign of my love
forever."

God called
Abraham:
"Leave your
house and go
towards the land
which I will
show you."
Abraham
obeyed God.
He left with
his wife Sarah,
his servants
and his flocks.
They walked
towards the
promised land.
God said to
Abraham,
"Your children's
children will be
as many as the
stars in the sky."

Abraham and Sarah thanked God.
They were full of joy. Sarah laughed: even though they were very old, a little baby had been born to them, just as God promised.
They called him Isaac.
When he grew up, Isaac had his own children.
They would become a great people.

Abraham's grandchildren, the Hebrews, were slaves of Pharaoh, the king of Egypt.

One day, Pharaoh's daughter went to bathe in the river. She saw a little Hebrew baby in a basket floating on the water.

She said to him, "You will be my child and you will be called Moses, because I saved you from the water."

Moses grew up.
God said to him,
"I am the Lord,
your God.
Lead the
Hebrews
out of Egypt,
because they are
very unhappy."
Moses obeyed
God. But Pharaoh
chased the
Hebrews
with his
army.
So God opened a
way through the
sea and saved his
people.

On the mountain, God spoke to Moses, "I am your only God. Love me with all your heart."
Moses carried the Word of God, written on two big stones which he put into a beautiful box: the Ark of the Covenant.
In this way God would always be present in the midst of his people who keep his word.

David was a little shepherd from Bethlehem.
There was a war. The giant Goliath shouted in his great voice, "Who will come and fight me? The strongest will win!"
Only David answered, "I will and I'm coming without a sword. I'm not afraid of you because God is with me!"
And God gave him the victory.

David became
a great king.
He sang and
danced for God
as the Ark
of the
Covenant
entered
Jerusalem:
"All the earth,
sing out your
joy to the Lord!
Alleluia!"
David's son,
King Solomon,
built a beautiful
house for God:
the Temple of
Jerusalem.

God called
Isaiah.
He answered,
"Here I am."
So God sent
him to say
to everyone,
"Prepare the way.
The Lord is
coming. A child
will be born and
he will bring joy
and peace.
The Spirit of
God will be upon
him. He will
gather together
all the peoples
of the earth,
and they will
walk
towards
his light."

A little baby was born in Bethlehem. His name was Jesus. He was the long-awaited Saviour, the promised Son of God. He was laid in a manger beside Mary and Joseph. The angels sang "Glory to God!" The shepherds were amazed. Heaven and earth rejoiced! It's Christmas!

As a child, Jesus lived in Nazareth with his mother, Mary and her husband Joseph, the carpenter. Joseph took care of the family that God had entrusted to him. Jesus grew in strength and wisdom. The Spirit of God was with him.

HOSANNA!

When Jesus was thirty years old, he travelled all around his country to tell everyone the Good News: "God is our Father. Love each other because you are all brothers." Jesus welcomed everyone who came to him, the poor and the humble. He forgave them and healed them.

Jesus gathered his friends for a meal.
He blessed the bread, broke it and gave it to them saying, "This is my body given for you. Take it and eat it." Jesus blessed the cup filled with wine and said "This is my blood, poured out for you. Take it and drink it."

In Jerusalem,
Jesus carried
the heavy cross.
He was
surrounded
by soldiers.
Mary, John,
and some friends
stayed with him.
People who didn't
believe Jesus
was the Son of
God, condemned
him to suffer and
die on the cross.
Jesus forgave
them. He gave
his life out of
love for all men.

alleluia!

Three days later,
on Easter
morning, Jesus
wasn't in the
tomb anymore.
Mary Magdalene
saw Jesus.
He was alive!
He had risen
from the dead!
What great joy!
Alleluia!
Jesus calls us to
a new life,
gathered
together in the
love of
God our
Father
for ever. Alleluia!

alleluia!

On the day of Pentecost, Jesus's friends were praying together with Mary. The Spirit of God came down on them like a wind, like a fire which transformed their hearts. And so they wanted to tell the Good News of the Love of God to all their brothers on the earth, "In the name of the Father, and of the Son, and of the Holy Spirit."

CTS Children's Books

The beautiful Story of Jesus, *by Maïte Roche*
(ISBN 978 1 86082 492 0 CTS Code CH 13)

Benedict & Chico, *by Jeanne Perego*
(ISBN 978 1 86082 493 7 CTS Code CH 12)

The Bible for little children, *by Maïte Roche*
(ISBN 978 1 86082 399 2 CTS Code CH 2)

Faith for children, *by Christine Pedotti*
(ISBN 978 1 86082 447 0 CTS Code CH 9)

First prayers for little children, *by Maïte Roche*
(ISBN 978 1 86082 443 2 CTS Code CH 5)

The Gospel for little children, *by Maïte Roche*
(ISBN 978 1 86082 400 5 CTS Code CH 1)

The most beautiful Christmas Story, *by Maïte Roche*
(ISBN 978 1 86082 446 3 CTS Code CH 8)

Prayers around the Crib, *by Juliette Levivier*
(ISBN 978 1 86082 445 6 CTS Code CH 7)

Praying at Mass, *by Juliette Levivier*
(ISBN 978 1 86082 491 3 CTS Code CH 11)

Praying with Mary, *by Juliette Levivier*
(ISBN 978 1 86082 536 1 CTS Code CH 14)

Praying with the Holy Spirit, *by Juliette Levivier*
(ISBN 978 1 86082 537 8 CTS Code CH 15)

Praying with the first Chritians, *by Juliette Levivier*
(ISBN 978 1 86082 490 6 CTS Code CH 10)

Praying with the friends of Jesus, *by Juliette Levivier*
(ISBN 978 1 86082 444 9 CTS Code CH 6)

The Rosary, *by Juliette Levivier*
(ISBN 978 1 86082 397 8 CTS Code CH 3)

The Way of the Cross, *by Juliette Levivier*
(ISBN 1 86082 398 X CTS Code CH 4)

The Bible for little children: Published 2006 by the Incorporated Catholic Truth Society, 40-46 Harleyford Road, London SE11 5AY. Tel: 020 7640 0042; Fax: 020 7640 0046; www.cts-online.org.uk. Copyright © 2006 the Incorporated Catholic Truth Society in this English language edition.

ISBN 978 1 86082 399 2   CTS Code CH 2

La Bible pour les petits: by Maïte Roche, published 2003 by Groupe Fleurus, 15-27 rue Moussorgski, 75018 Paris; ISBN 2 7289 1056 1. Copyright © Groupe Fleurus 2003.